WILDLIFE MAZES

Roger Moreau

Sterling Publishing Co., Inc.

New York

**This book is dedicated to
Alex, Andrew, Brian, Austin,
Krista, Max, Lauren, David, and Kathren**

10 9 8 7 6 5 4 3 2 1

Published by Sterling Publishing Co., Inc.

387 Park Avenue South, New York, NY 10016

© 2005 by Roger Moreau

Distributed in Canada by Sterling Publishing

^{c}/o Canadian Manda Group, 165 Dufferin Street

Toronto, Ontario, Canada M6K 3H6

Distributed in Great Britain and Europe by Chris Lloyd at Orca Book

Services, Stanley House, Fleets Lane, Poole BH15 3AJ, England

Distributed in Australia by Capricorn Link (Australia) Pty. Ltd.

P.O. Box 704, Windsor, NSW 2756, Australia

Printed in China

All rights reserved

Sterling ISBN 1-4027-1552-8

Contents

Suggested Use of This Book

As you work your way through the pages of this book, try not to mark them. This will enable you to experience these adventures over and over again and will also give your friends a chance to see if they have the same skills and amount of courage that you have.

Special Warning: When the way looks too difficult, avoid the temptation to start at the end and work your way backwards. This technique would be a violation of the rules and could result in tragedy.

Cover Maze: Here is a chance to get some great photos of a variety of wildlife. Find a clear path to that elephant in the distance. You can cross rocks and logs.

Introduction

The diversity of life on this earth is very extensive. On each of the seven continents (Europe, Antarctica, Asia, Africa, Australia, North America, South America), the wildlife is unique and different. For example, the wildlife that exists on the African continent (elephants, giraffes, gorillas, and rhinoceros) is different than the wildlife in Asia. The wildlife that lives on these two continents does not appear on the South and North American continents. There is wildlife in South America that is not found in North America, and vice versa. Just to name a few, the jaguar and anaconda can be found in South America, and the grizzly bear, bobcat, and elk are found only in North America. None of these species appear on any of the other continents. The same kinds of examples are true with the remaining three continents: Australia, Antarctica, and Europe.

Wouldn't it be exciting to go on a safari and photograph the different species of wildlife on these continents? It certainly would. So pack your gear and get ready to go. It will be difficult to travel to all of the continents in one safari, so we'll pick out Africa and Asia to get started and end up in South and North America. That should give a pretty good selection of the unique and different varieties of wildlife in the world.

This safari will probably be dangerous. You're going to need a lot of courage. Many of the animals you'll try to take photos of can attack. You'll want to get as close to the subject as possible and, if the subject desires to eat you, do not retreat in fear before you get the photo. It might be advisable to wear a good pair of running shoes. Good luck and have a great safari!

Safari Plans

Africa and Asia

You will be starting your safari on the continent of Africa, where you will be riding in a custom-built 4 x 4 vehicle built to drive over the rugged terrain of the Nairobi National Park. You will be entering a vast area alive with many different kinds of wildlife. It will be difficult to choose which animals to photograph. Some are endangered species, like the first one you will see up close, the black rhino. While in Africa, be ready to climb up vines, run over rough trails, and cross rivers to get great photos.

You'll have the chance to visit Asia, where there will be cobras, orangutans, gorillas, and even the rare panda. Again, your abilities will be required to get the best photo. Just be careful, because the wildlife here doesn't understand that they are safe. To them, *you* could present a danger. If that happens, get out of their way fast!

South and North America

Begin your South American safari at the tip of the continent, Tierra Del Fuego, where you will encounter some Magellanic penguins. You'll have to risk your life to photograph the endangered jaguar and, when you get to North America, watch out for the grizzly bear. Finish this great safari experience near the Arctic Circle and photograph the wonderful polar bears you will find there.

Take plenty of film for a regular camera, and have a digital camera on hand just as a backup. Who knows, the Nobel prize for photography could be yours.

Get Ready to Go

Load up the camera equipment by finding a clear path to the safari car.

End

Start

African Outback

Drive to the valley in the distance by finding a clear road.

Start

End

Black Rhino

Take a photo of this charging black rhino and escape by finding a clear path to the valley in the distance.

Start

End

Climb the Vines

Find your way up these vines to the top and continue up so that you can photograph the giraffe. Do not cross onto a connecting vine.

Start

Giraffe

On the same vine from the previous page, continue up to the tree limb and photograph the giraffe.

End

Charging Elephants

Get a photo of each one of these charging elephants by finding a clear path to each one and escape.

Start

End

Lion and Snake

Photograph this charging lion and escape up those vines. Be careful to avoid the poisonous African Gaboon snake and the spider. Do not cross onto a connecting vine.

Start

End

Nile Crocodiles

Cross the stream on the connecting rocks to photograph that big croc on the other side and escape to the sandbar on the right.

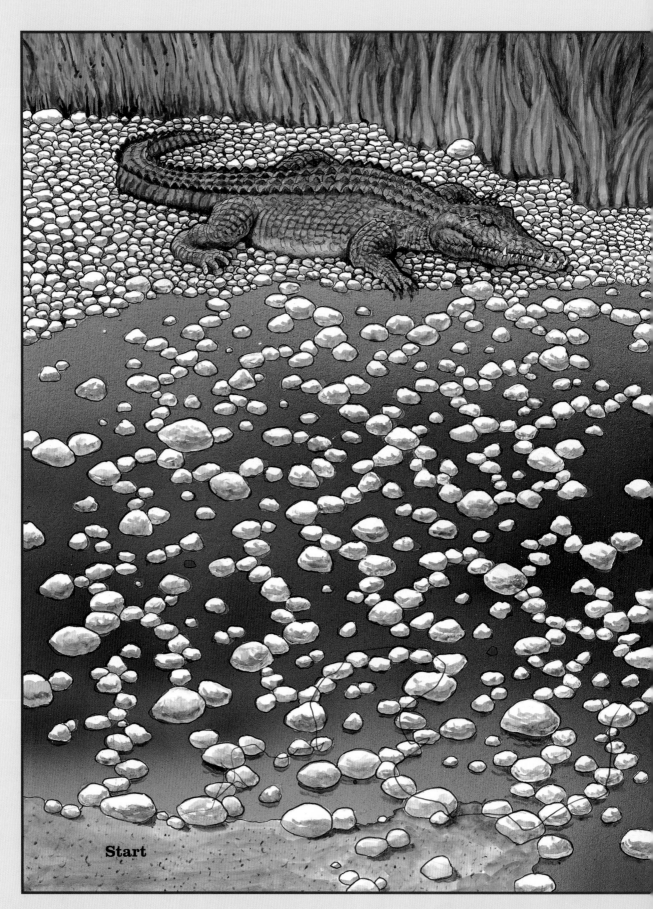

Start

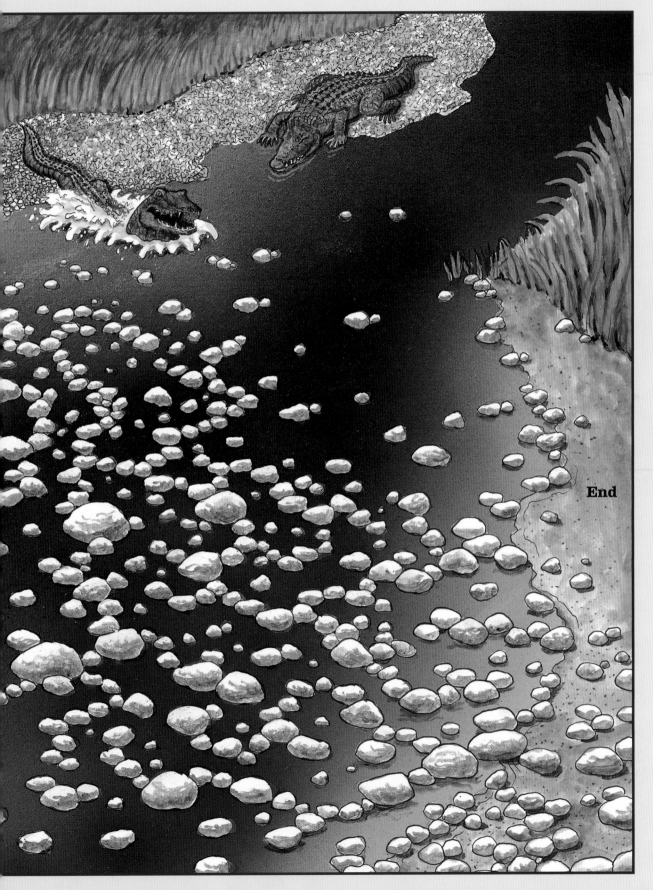

End

Geometric Tortoises

Find your way to photograph the two geometric tortoises by descending the path to the rocks and climbing down the connecting rocks to the tortoises.

Start

End

King Cobra

The first creature you'll encounter in Asia is a very dangerous one: the king cobra. Start anywhere at the top. Do not disturb the baby cobras and find a clear path to get a close-up photo of the mother.

Orangutan

Start on the vines at the left and continue to the vine nearest the orangutan to get a close-up photo. Do not cross onto a connecting vine.

Start

End

Pandas

Find a clear path around the bamboo plants to the mother panda to photograph her.

Start

End

Gorillas

Cross the streams on the fallen logs to the gorillas on the other side. You can step over branches but nothing else.

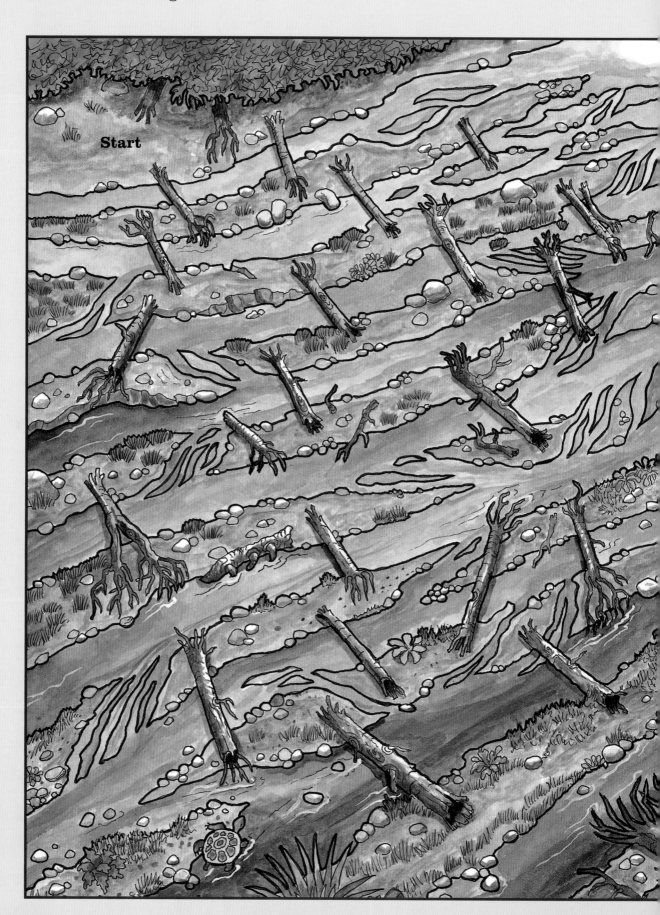

Start

End

Komodo Dragon

Find a clear path to photograph the dragon and escape to the upper right.

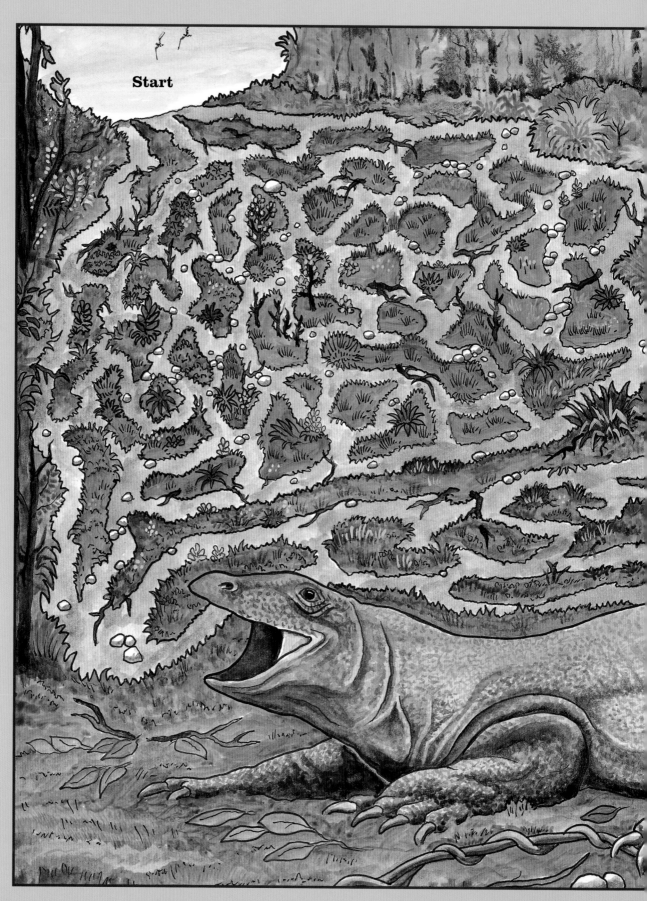

Start

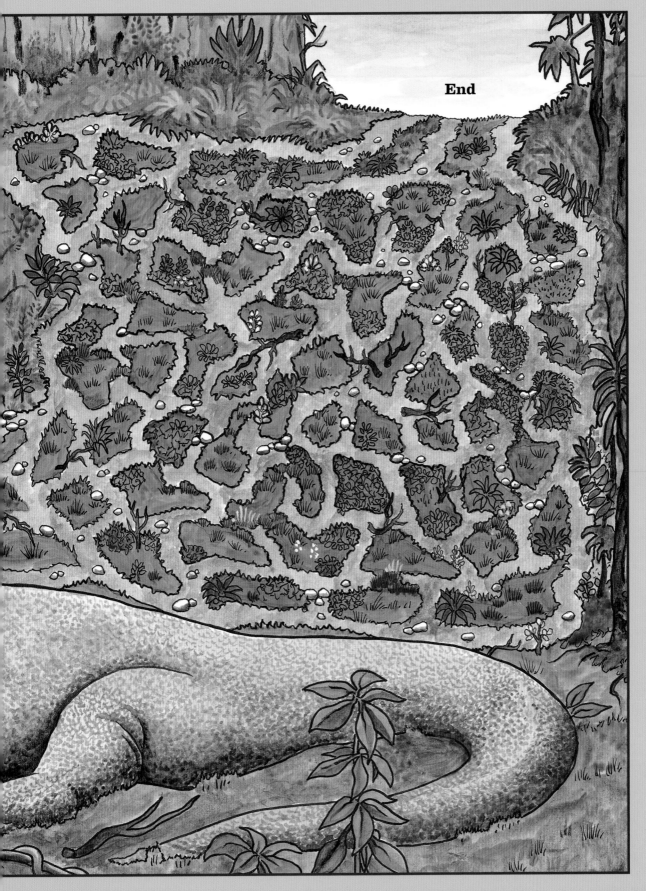

End

Magellanic Penguins

The Magellanic penguins are the first creatures you'll encounter on your South America trip. Make your way carefully from the top of the ridge to the family below.

Start

End

Sleeping Armadillo

Find a clear path and photograph the sleeping armadillo.

Start

End

Anaconda

Avoid the water lilies and the South American anaconda and swim to photograph the snake's head.

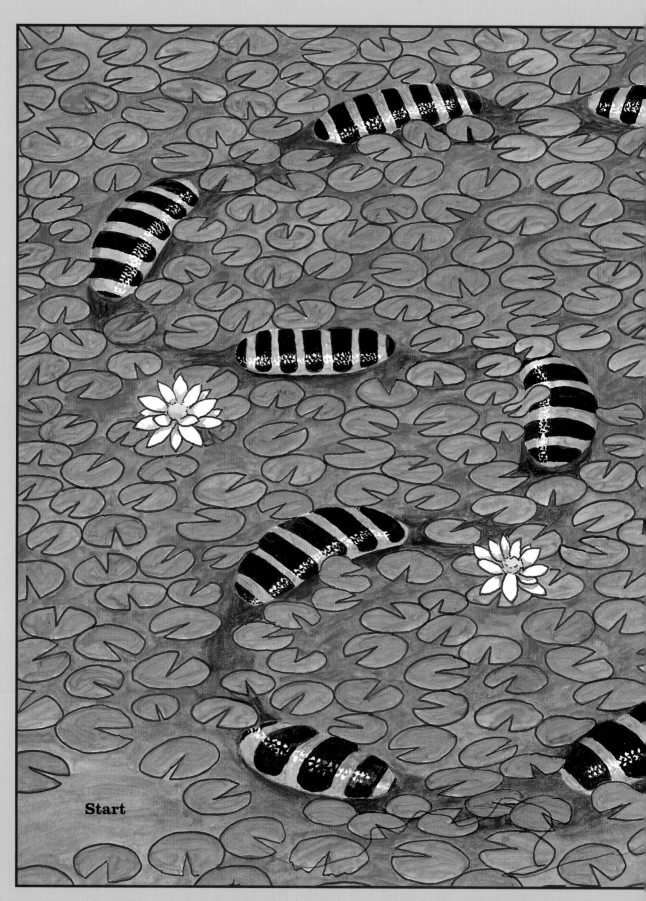

Start

End

Piranha and Jaguar

Walk through the shallow waters of the stream, avoiding the piranha and everything else to photograph the jaguar.

Start

End

Diamondback and Gila Monster

Welcome to North America! Find a clear path to get a photo of the gila monster and the diamondback rattlesnake before they do battle.

Start

End

End

Teton Elk

You are now in the Teton range—a mountain front. Find a clear path to the bull elk. You can cross the stream on rocks and fallen logs. You cannot cross over branches.

Start

End

Bobcat

Find a clear snow trail and hike up to the bobcat. Get a photo.

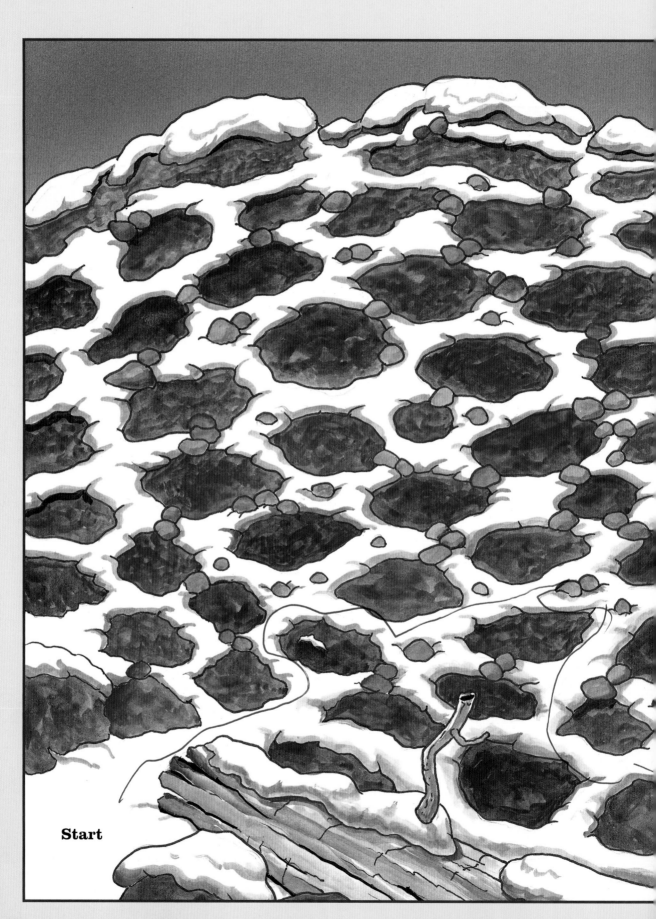

Start

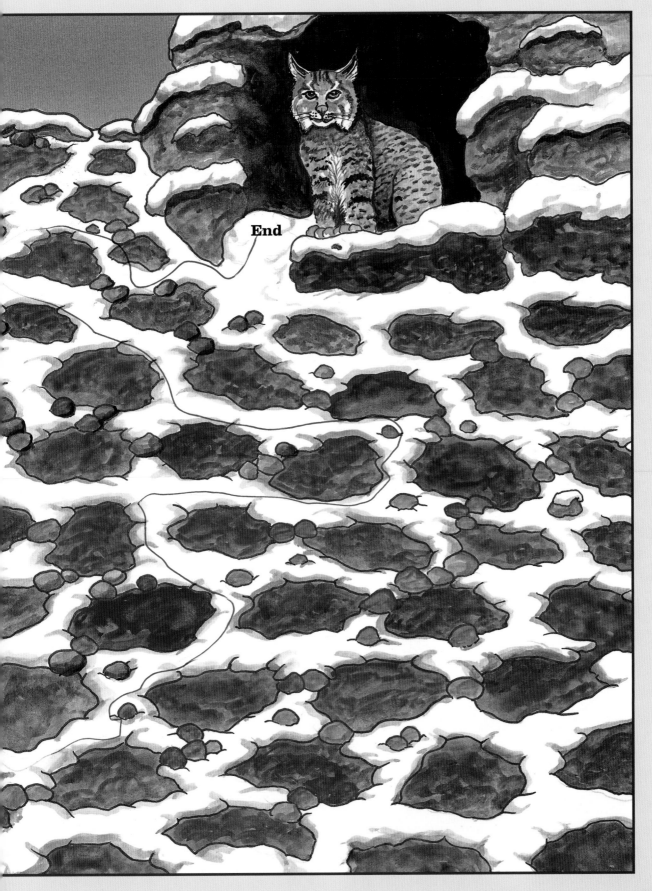

End

Yellowstone Moose

Avoid the hot thermal pools in Yellowstone National Park and find a clear path to the bull moose.

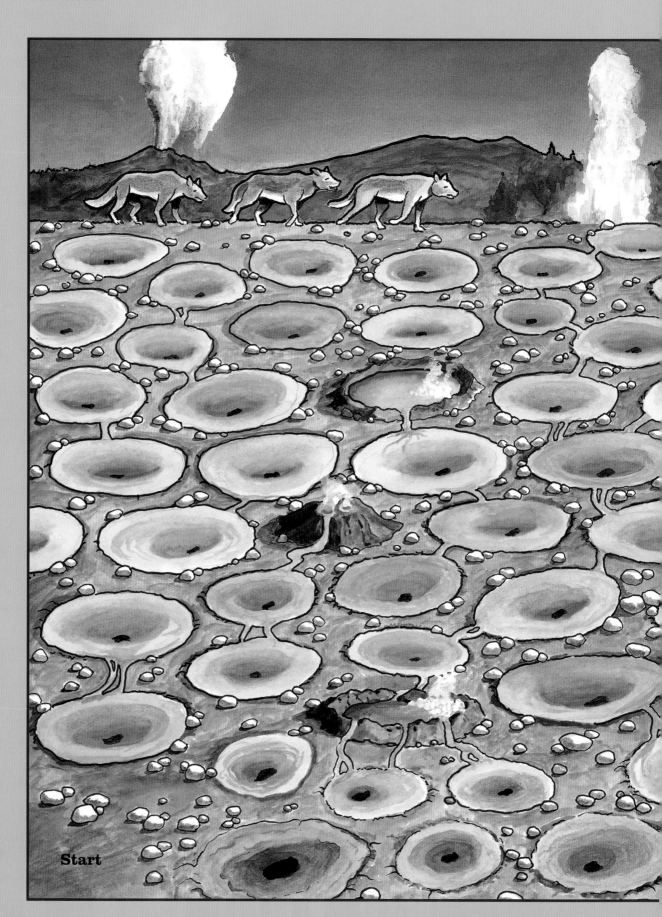

Start

End

Bighorn Sheep

Find a clear path to the top of the ridge and photograph the bighorn sheep before they run away.

Red Fox

Start anywhere at the top and find a clear path to photograph this red fox family.

Start

End

Grizzly Bear

Walk on the overlapping branches and logs to get a photo of that snarling grizzly bear.

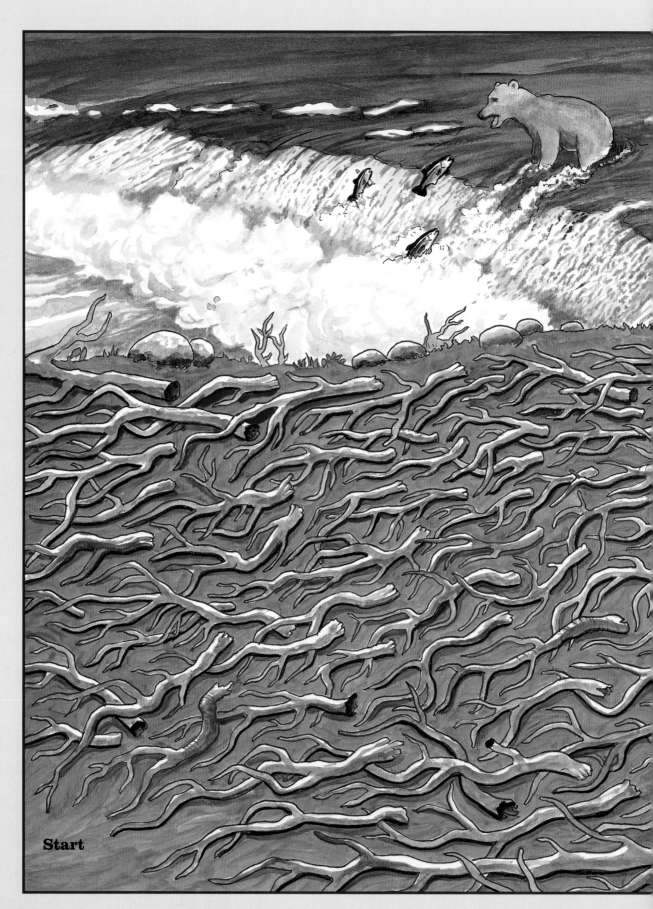

Start

End

Killer Whale

Hurry to the location of this event of nature, the feeding of a killer whale. Find a clear path.

Start

End

Polar Bears

Find a clear path on the ice blocks to photograph the polar bear family as they pass by.

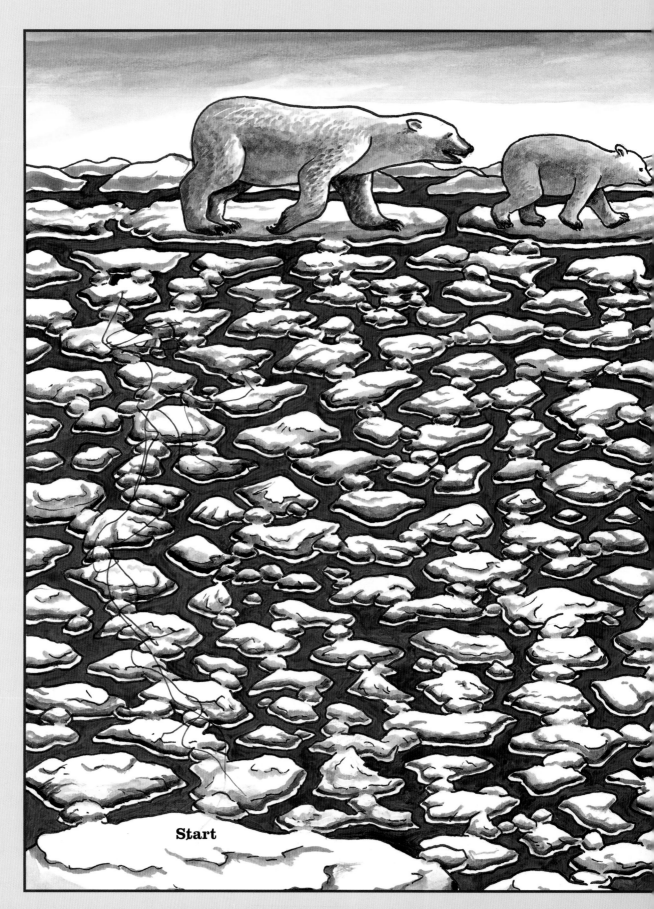

Start

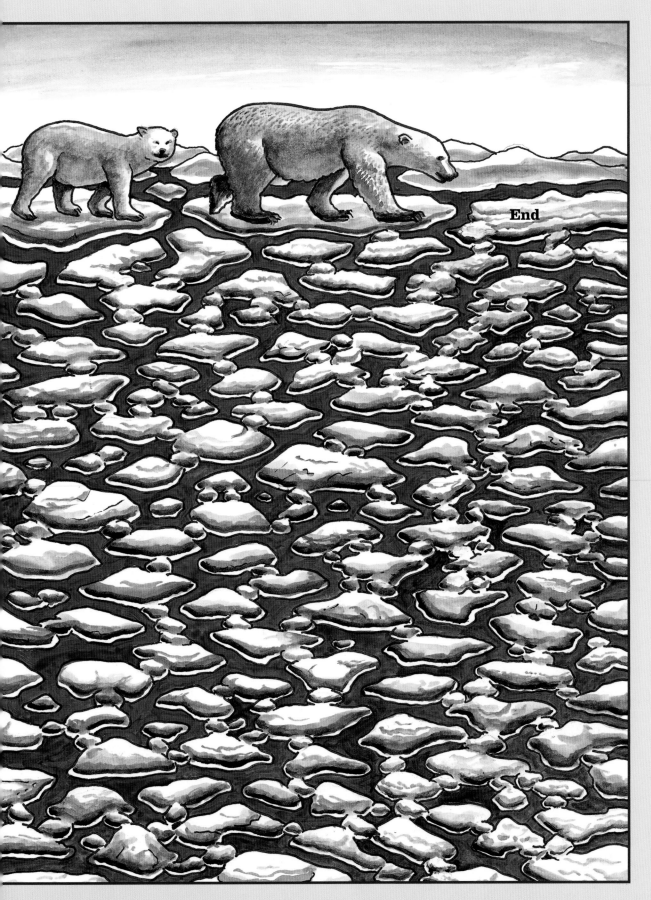

End

NOBEL PRIZE
Award

This award is presented to

for outstanding achievement in:

Wildlife Photography

Alfred Nobel
President

Youthe Best
Vice President

Congratulations!

Your photography work is outstanding and deserving of the Nobel prize for photography. Just fill in your name on the certificate above. Along with that great award should be an acknowledgment for the courage and perseverance that it took to get such wonderful photos. Nice going. Not everyone could achieve what you have achieved. Your future looks bright. You will be a great success in all that you do. You have proved that here.

If you had problems with any of the mazes, their solutions are on the following pages.

Cover Maze/Get Ready to Go

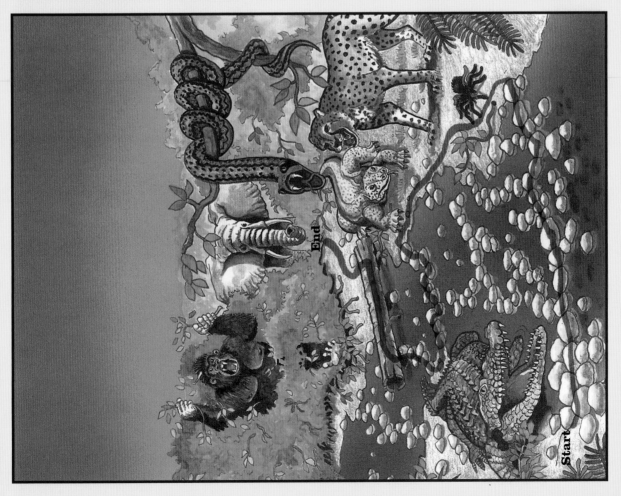

African Outback

Start

End

Black Rhino

Start

End

Climb the Vines

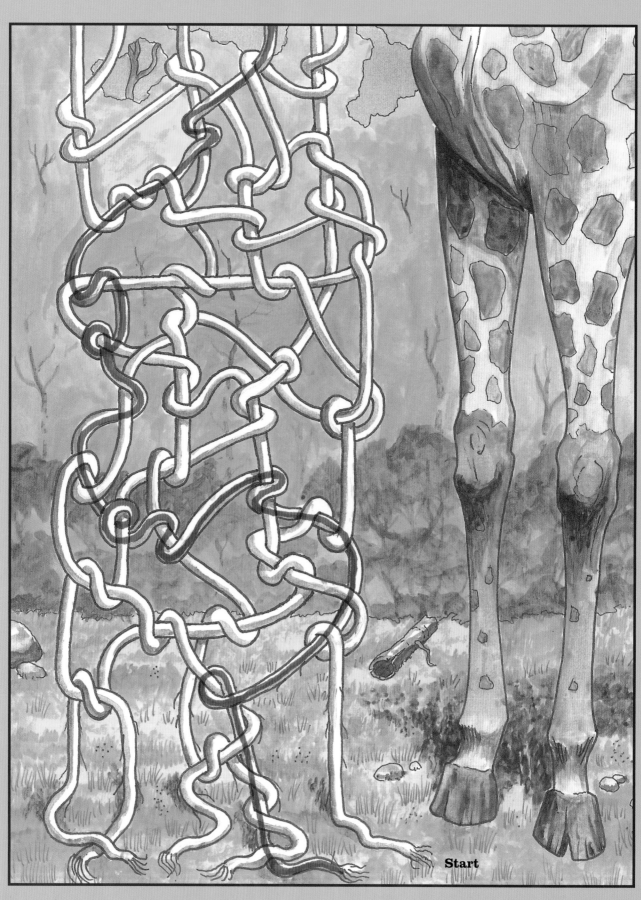

Start

Giraffe

End

Charging Elephants

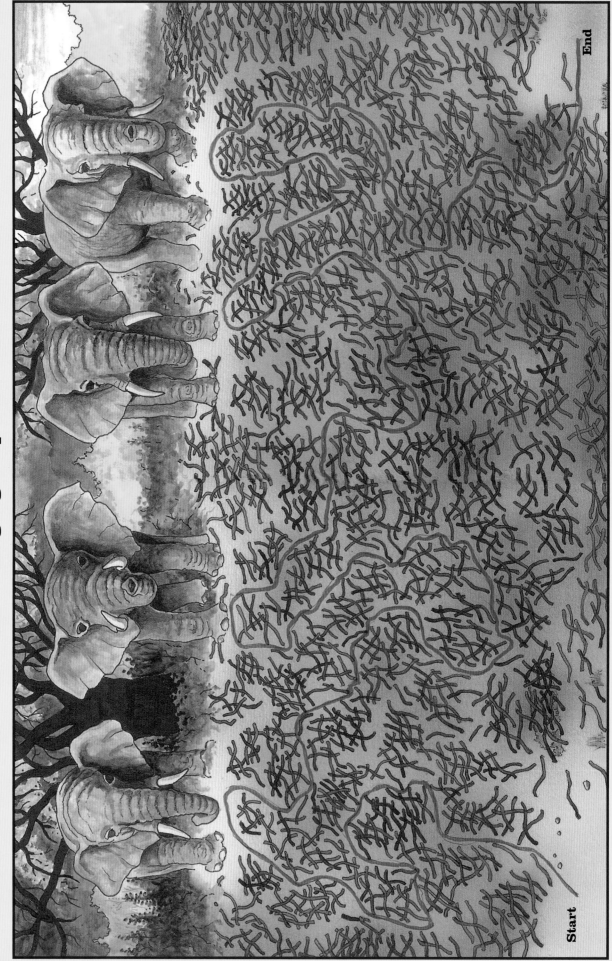

Start

End

Lion and Snake

End

Start

59

Nile Crocodiles

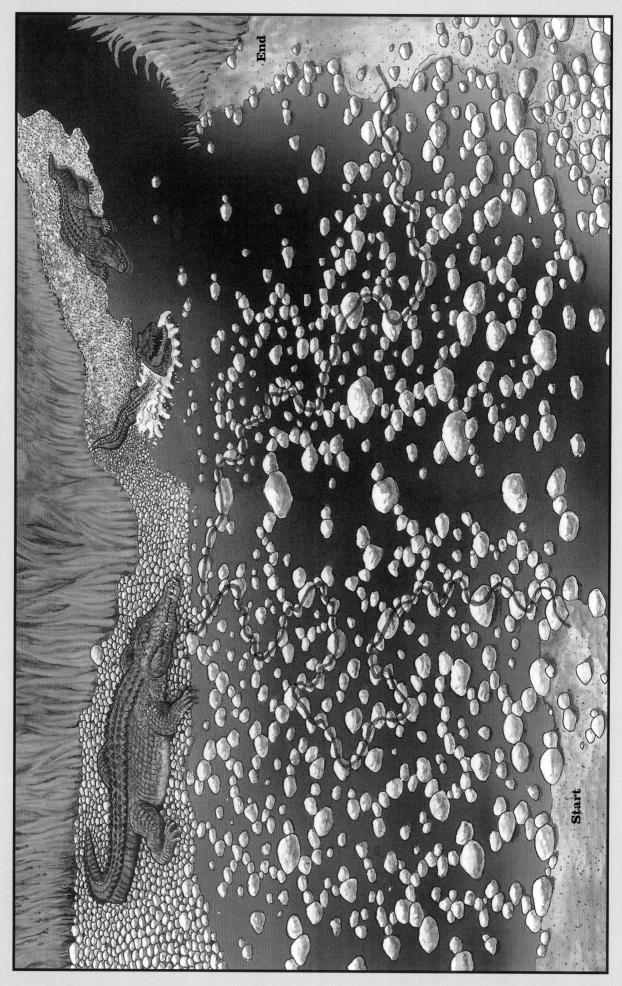

End

Start

60

Geometric Tortoises

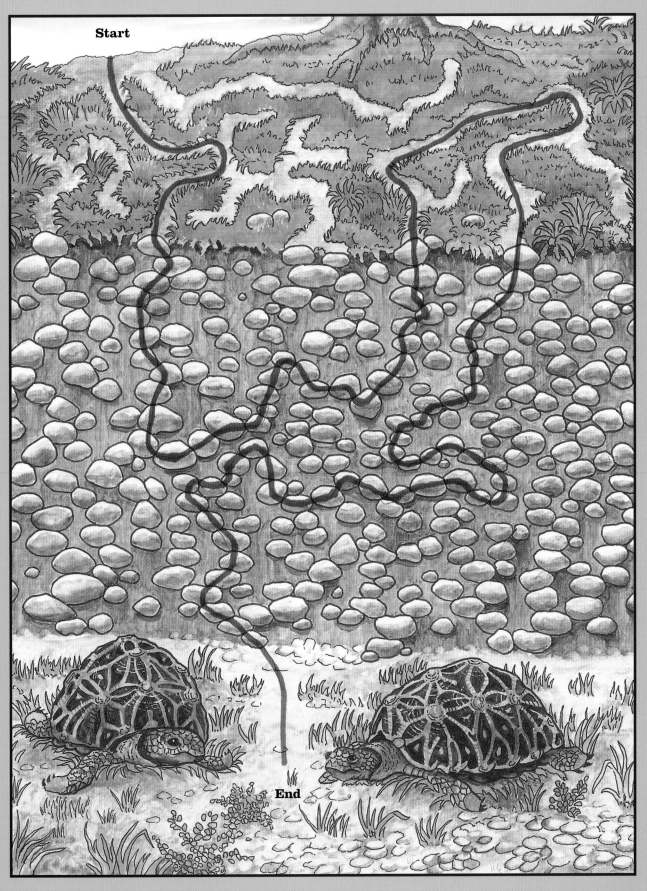

Start

End

King Cobra

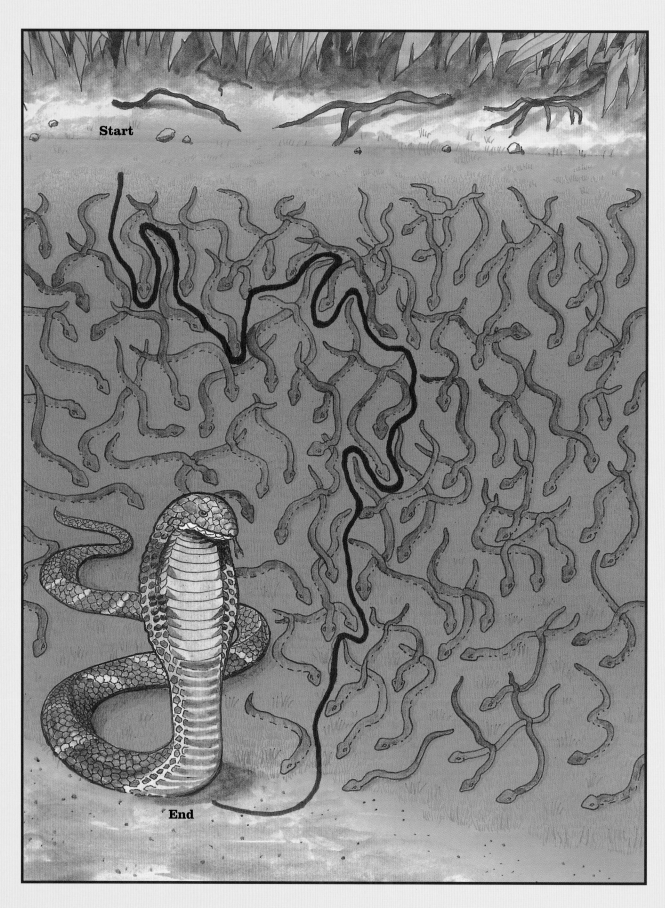

Start

End

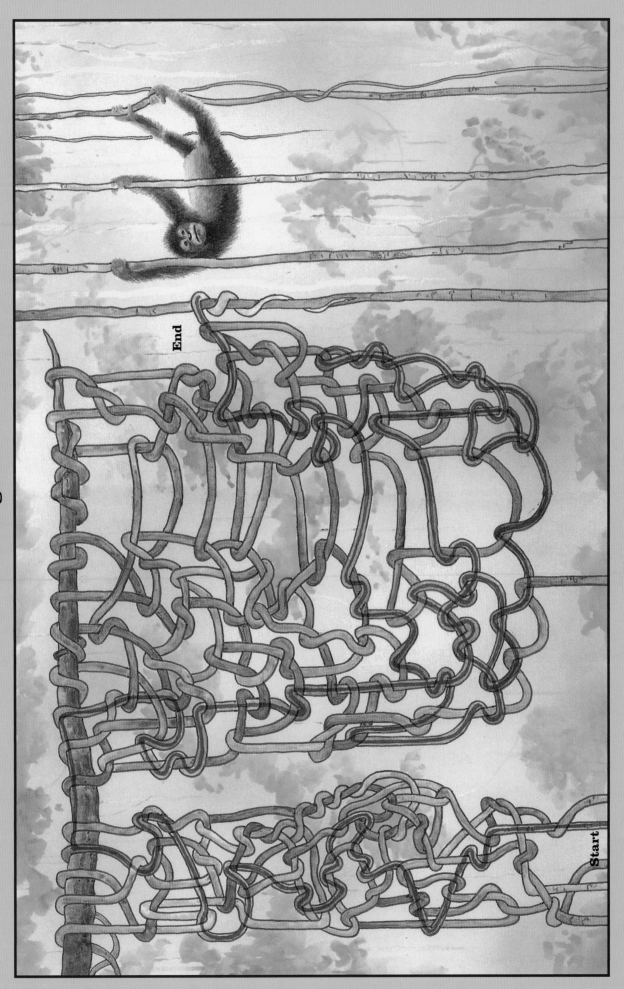

Orangutan

End

Start

63

Pandas

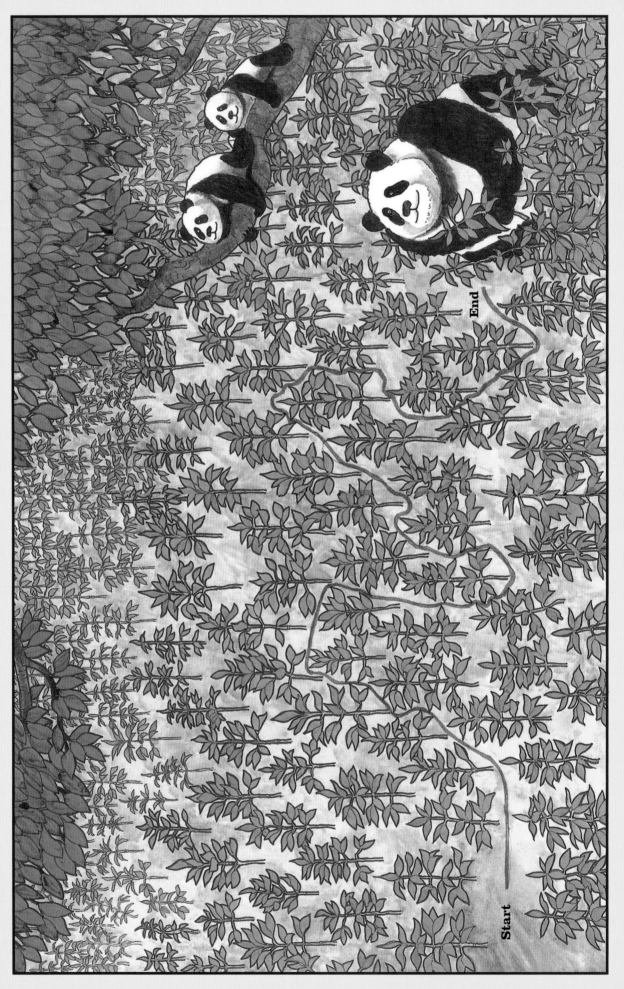

End

Start

64

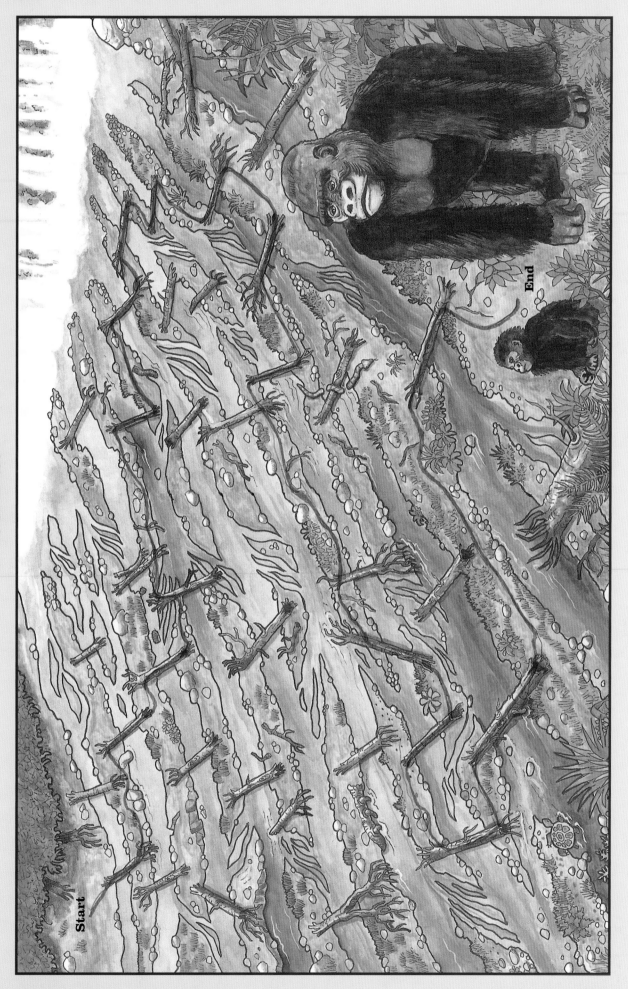

Gorillas

Start

End

65

Komodo Dragon

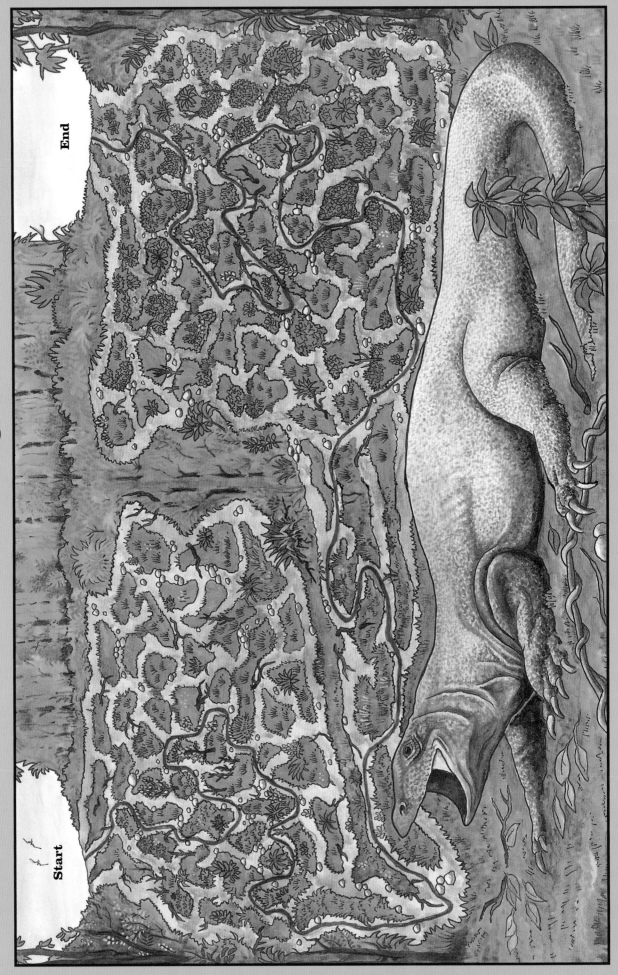

Start

End

66

Magellanic Penguins

Start

End

Sleeping Armadillo

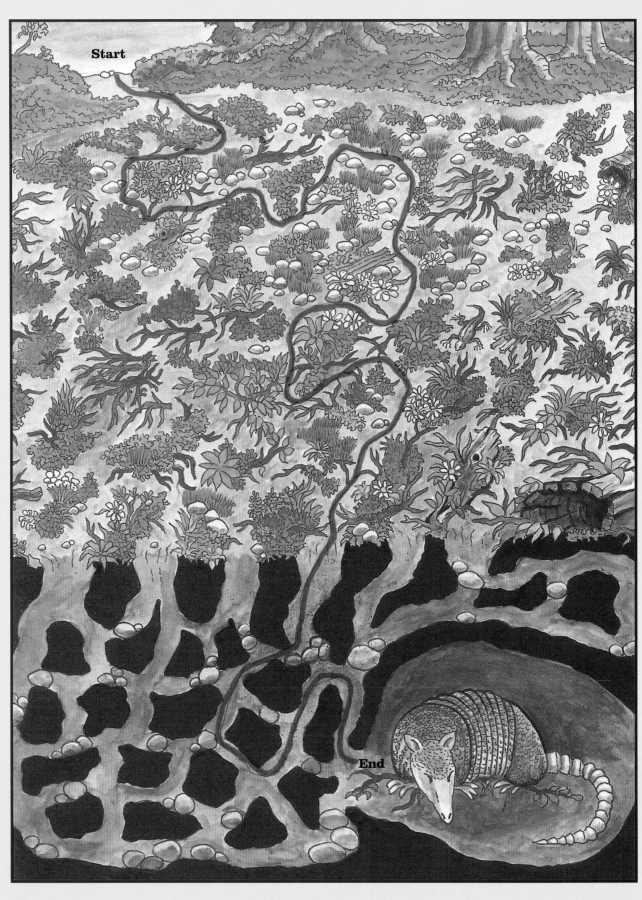

Start

End

Anaconda

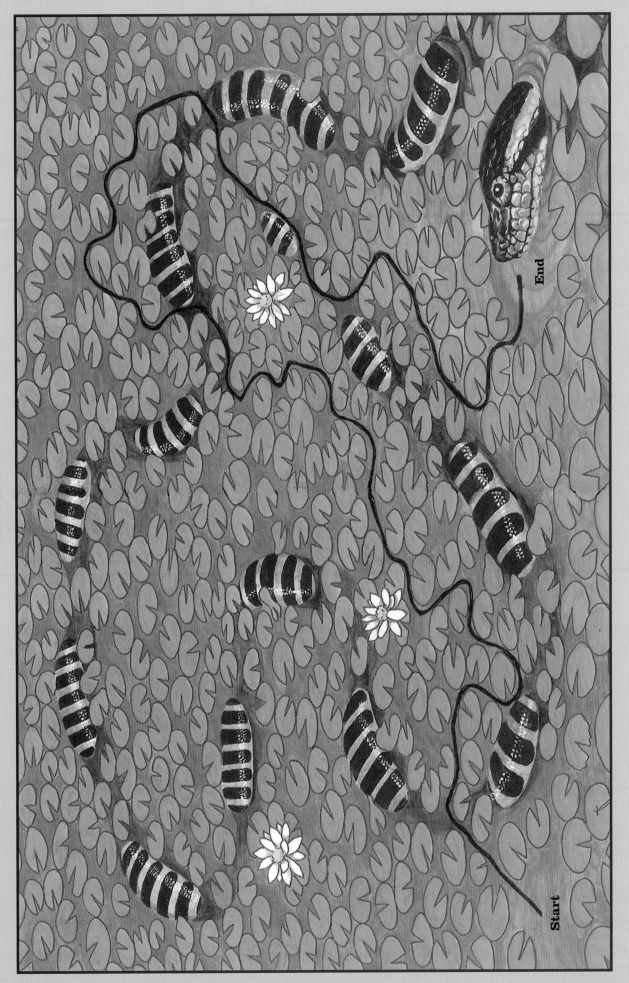

Start

End

69

Piranha and Jaguar

End

Start

70

Diamondback and Gila Monster

Start

End

71

Teton Elk

End

Start

Bobcat

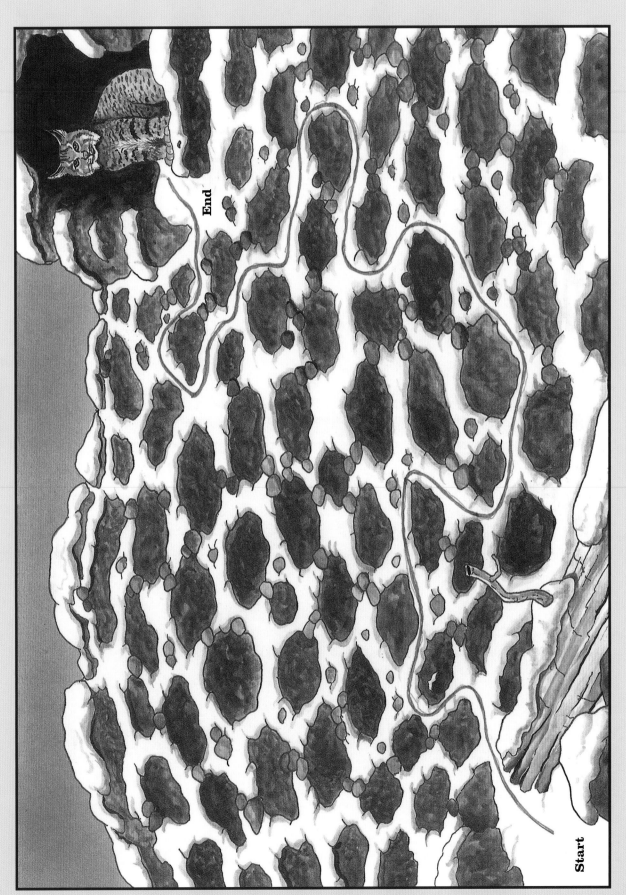

End

Start

73

Yellowstone Moose

End

Start

74

Bighorn Sheep

End

Start

Red Fox

Start

End

76

Grizzly Bear

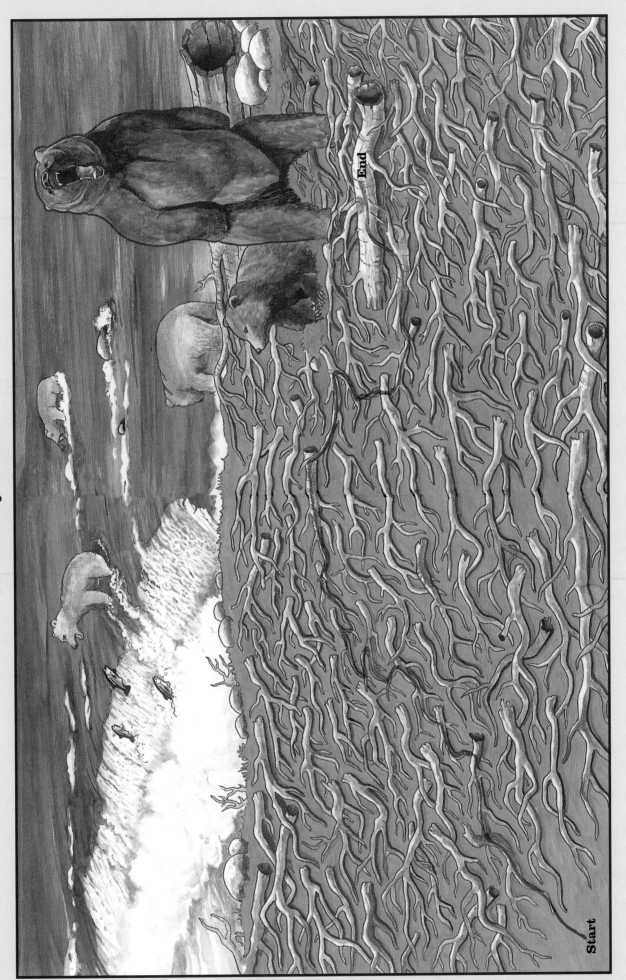

Start

End

Killer Whale

End

Start

78